PAPERCRAFT

STYLISH & SIMPLE

PAPERCRAFT

CLARE LOUISE HUNT

AURUM PRESS

First published in 1998 by
Aurum Press Ltd
25 Bedford Avenue
London WC1B 3AT

Conceived and produced by Breslich & Foss Ltd
20 Wells Mews
London W1P 3FJ

Project editor: Janet Ravenscroft
Designer: Janet James
Illustrator: Kevin Hart
All photography by Shona Wood, except
pages 17, 25, 38, 48-9 and 50 by David Armstrong

A catalogue record for this book is available from the British Library

ISBN 1 85410 557 4

Printed and bound in Hong Kong

Contents

Introduction 10

Introduction

Try to imagine a world without paper. If you stop to give it a moment's thought you will soon realise just how much we take paper for granted. It is part of our daily lives from the moment we awake to the time we go to bed.

Our correspondence is still largely dependent on paper, despite our living in the electronic era, and the daily news comes printed on sheets of it. We use paper money to buy food, much of which comes wrapped in layers of paper. We eat off paper plates, and drink from paper cups. At home we read books by the light of a paper lampshade. In short, paper is an essential and integral part of our lives and has been for centuries.

Not only has paper always had an essentially functional role, it has long had decorative and artistic purposes. Museums and galleries the world over are brimming with fascinating and priceless works of art in which paper, in its countless guises, forms the basic medium.

The earliest paper is thought to have been made as long ago as 3500 BC from a reed known as papyrus. This very basic paper was made by layering strips of the reed on flat stone slabs, then beating and pressing the layers so they dried with a smooth surface.

Later, the Chinese developed a new method in which all manner of raw materials were boiled up to form a pulp. A mesh was drawn through the pulp, and the result was a layer of intermingled fibres that was then dried and pressed to form a thin sheet. As you will discover, it is easy to create your own paper using this traditional method.

Most of the paper seen today is produced using sophisticated machine methods. These give us a wide range of graded papers from the fine, coated variety to the uniformly coarse and textured quality art papers. But handmade papers are available from shops and, though more expensive than standard manufactured papers, they never fail to lend a special charm to decorative projects.

The projects in this book cover numerous techniques related to papercrafts and use many kinds of papers, both handmade and manufactured. Working with paper is immensely rewarding and enjoyable, whether you are making handmade flower papers, block printing, making and decorating books, or designing party invitations and decorations. I hope that making the projects in this book will inspire you to create your own designs.

MAKING AND DECORATING PAPER

Paper Making

Making your own paper is great fun and not as difficult as you might imagine. The step-by-step instructions and diagrams are there to guide you, and you will soon discover which effects you like best. Few materials are needed: a mould and deckle (see page 22), a large container and a blender are the most essential. The paper itself can be made from all kinds of everyday things. Begin by experimenting with wastepaper – anything from used envelopes to yesterday's newspaper – then let your imagination run wild, adding petals, leaves, or gold stars.

It is hard to give precise quantities for the pulp, but in consistency it should be like a thin porridge. Begin by tearing a few sheets of paper into small scraps and placing them in a blender. Fill almost to the top with cold water. Blend until the paper has disintegrated and the mixture is smooth. The average blender holds about 1 litre (2 pints) of water, so you will have to prepare the pulp in batches, pouring each batch into the container as it is finished. As a result, it is easy to adjust the consistency of the paper pulp as you go.

Different mixtures will give you different papers. Even those that 'go wrong' will have their own charm, so experiment and have fun!

MATERIALS YOU WILL NEED

Wastepaper
Blender
Large plastic container
Wooden spoon
Mould and deckle
Kitchen cloths
Indoor line and pegs

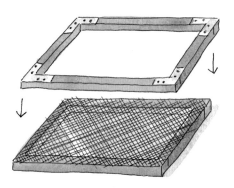

1 Place the deckle over the mould, keeping the mesh side of the mould uppermost.

2 Stir the pulp vigorously. Plunge the short side of the frame vertically into the vat then hold it flat under the water.

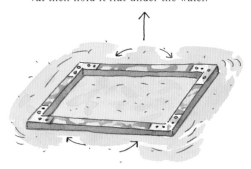

3 Still holding the frame flat, bring it up through the water, shaking it from side to side to spread the pulp evenly.

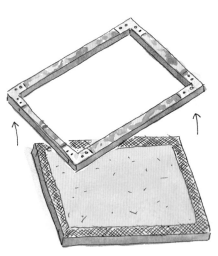

4 Lift the frame, keeping it flat, and let the water drain back into the vat. Place the mould carefully on a flat surface and lift the deckle away.

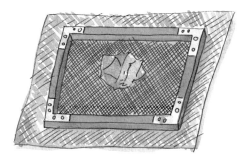

5 When the excess water has drained from the paper, carefully turn the mould paper side down and lay it flat on a damp kitchen cloth. The paper will stick to the mesh. Blot the paper through the mesh with a dry cloth before carefully removing the mould. Lift one side then the other in a gentle rocking motion to release the paper from the mesh.

6 Lift the damp kitchen cloth with the paper attached and pin to an indoor clothes line. Leave until almost dry, then sandwich between two dry kitchen cloths and place under a pile of heavy books or magazines.

Gold and silver stars added to the pulp lend a nice festive feel to plain white paper. You can also add flecks of silver and gold cut from a larger sheet of paper, or from sweet wrappers. Glitter added to a fine pulp produces a delightful paper.

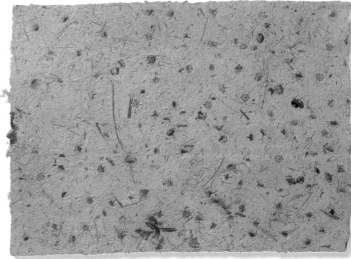

Some lovely patterns can be achieved by adding plant material, such as leaves, flower heads, petals, or even plant and vegetable fibre, to the paper pulp. Some plants, such as onions and beetroots, add beautiful colours to the paper. Simply chop one up and whiz it in the blender with paper pulp. If you are using flower heads, you can either suspend them in the pulp, or drop them on to the pulp just after lifting the deckle from the vat (see page 18, Step 3). The latter gives you more control over how the flowers are distributed on the paper.

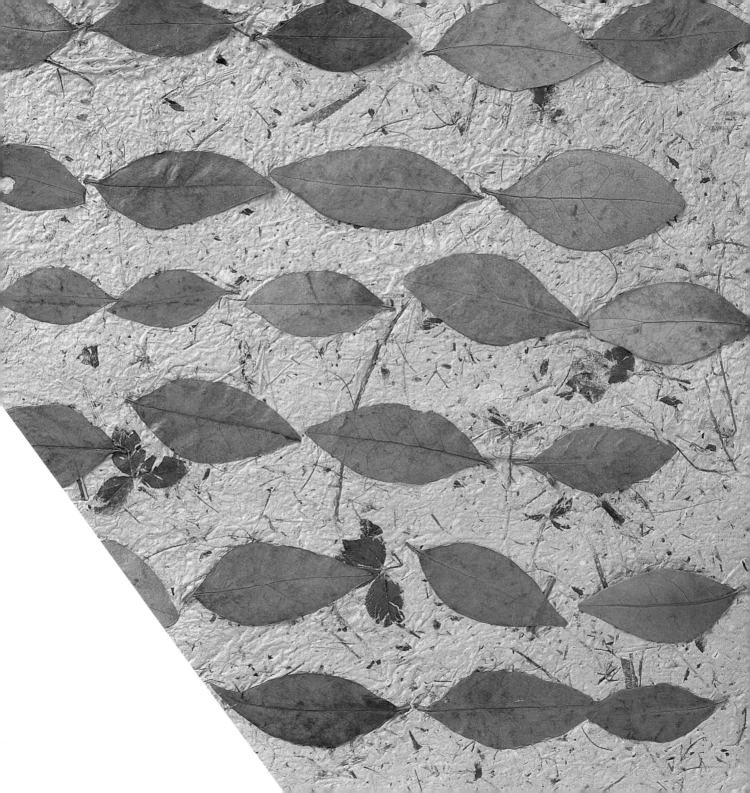

Mould and Deckle

Moulds and deckles are available from paper-making specialists, but it is very easy to make your own. Use two wooden picture frames that are exactly the same size. Try to find frames that are not painted or varnished. The main advantage of making your own frame is that you can decide how large or small it should be.

As the mould will be repeatedly soaked in water, it is important to use metallic materials that won't rust. Hardware shops stock a variety of brass screws and nails, and you can find aluminium mesh in car accessory shops.

MATERIALS YOU WILL NEED

2 plain wooden frames
8 L-shaped braces
Screws
Screw-driver
Wire mesh
Nails

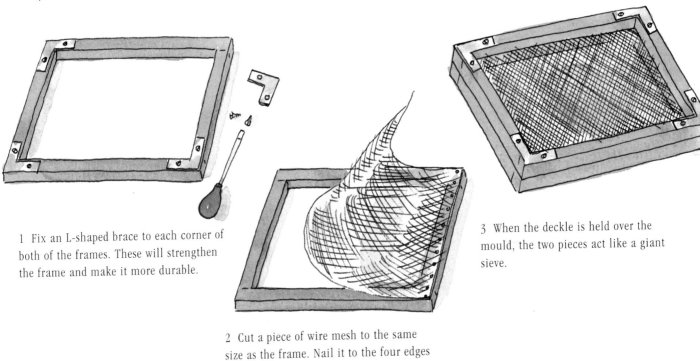

1 Fix an L-shaped brace to each corner of both of the frames. These will strengthen the frame and make it more durable.

2 Cut a piece of wire mesh to the same size as the frame. Nail it to the four edges with brass nails.

3 When the deckle is held over the mould, the two pieces act like a giant sieve.

Printing

Printing is great fun, very easy, and a wonderful way to add a personal touch to homemade or bought papers. Use printed handmade paper to make cards and lighter-weight paper to wrap gifts.

My favourite printing method is to use vegetables such as potatoes and swedes, which are widely available, inexpensive, and easy to sculpt. Swede blocks will last longer than potato blocks and you can keep them overnight as long as you keep the cut side face down on a plate to prevent it from drying out. You can also get interesting shapes from hard fruits, such as apples. Whatever you use, it is important to keep the printing surface as flat as possible to ensure an even coverage of ink or paint.

MATERIALS YOU WILL NEED

Paper
Marker pen
Vegetables
Knife
Sandpaper
Paints
Old plate
Newspapers

1 Draw your design on a piece of paper with a marker pen. Cut a large swede or potato in half, dry it, then sandpaper the surface completely flat. Place the design ink side down on the cut surface of the vegetable. When you remove the paper, a faint ink impression will remain.

2 Cut away the vegetable flesh, leaving only the design in relief on the flat surface. Lay the paper you wish to decorate on a thick layer of newspapers. Dip the vegetable block into the paint, then press it down on the printing surface. Repeat until the design is finished and leave to dry.

Spattering

Spattering is a very quick and easy way to achieve interesting results with plain paper. Before you begin, protect the work surface with a wide layer of newspaper. You will need a hard-bristled brush (an old toothbrush would do fine), and paints mixed to the correct consistency. Practice spattering on to scrap paper before you start. Run your thumb over the head of the brush so that a mist of droplets falls on to the page. Repeat using different colours until you are satisfied with the result. Spattering on tissue paper is especially effective as the paint will mix and blend with the colours of the damp tissue.

MATERIALS YOU WILL NEED

Oil paints or watercolours
White spirit
Stiff brush
Plain or tissue paper

1 Mix up the colours you are going to use. If using oils, add a little white spirit; if using watercolours, add a little water. The consistency should not be too thick or it will not spatter, or too thin as it will run.

2 Dip your brush into the first colour. Hold it over the paper and draw your thumb over the bristles towards you. (If you are concerned about getting your hands dirty, wear rubber gloves.) The paint will spatter on to the sheet of paper.

3 Repeat as often as necessary, changing the tone, or using a second and third colour as required.

Stencilling

Stencilling is an extremely versatile technique that offers an alternative to printing, while producing a similar effect. Instead of cutting a block and stamping the pattern on to the paper, ink or paint is sponged through a card or acetate stencil. Stencilling allows you to produce intricate shapes by cutting delicate patterns with a craft knife.

MATERIALS YOU WILL NEED

Stencilling acetate
Marker pen
Scissors or craft knife
Plain paper
Paint
Sponge or stencilling brush

1 Trace the design on to a sheet of stencilling acetate using a marker pen. Taking great care not to nip your fingertips, cut out the shape you have drawn.

2 Place the stencil on the paper that you wish to decorate. Apply the paint using a sponge or stencilling brush. Dab on the paint sparingly so that it does not run under the stencil.

3 Carefully lift the stencil off the paper and leave to dry before using it again. If it is not completely dry when you re-use it, paint may smudge on to the clean sheet of paper.

Marbling

The effect produced by floating oil-based paints on water then transferring the paint to paper is known as marbling because the result has the veiny quality of marble. You can use any paper, so long as it isn't too absorbent.

The simplest marbling technique is shown here, but you can use combs, feathers and special paint-dispersing liquids to produce more sophisticated results. You will soon establish what works well and what appeals to you. Mixing colours is great fun, but single colours and simple patterns can be equally striking.

1 Fill the container with cold water. Decide on your colour scheme and mix a little paint with white spirit. Add a small amount of the paint mix to the surface of the water with a pipette or paintbrush.

2 Use a spoon or a stick to swirl the paint into interesting patterns. If you wish, you can use a wide comb to create a more structured effect.

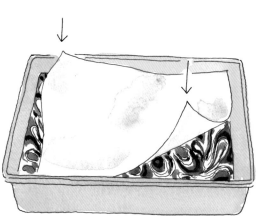

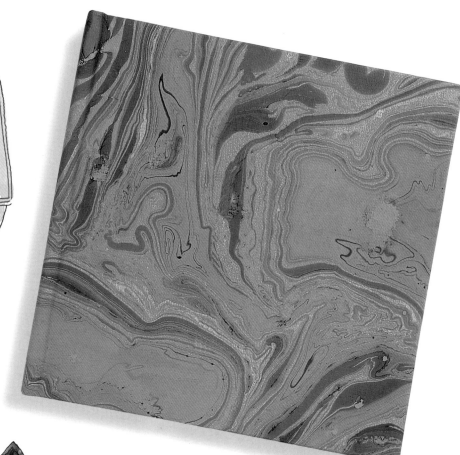

3 Gently lay a piece of paper on the surface of the water, holding the two opposite corners and lowering the middle of the paper first.

4 Carefully lift the paper out of the water and place it paint side up on a thick layer of newspaper. Leave to dry.

Papier mâché Frame

If you have an old and rather boring frame, don't throw it out: transform it into this rococo wonder. Papier mâché is easily made by soaking small pieces of paper in a mixture of wallpaper paste and water. Once you have placed a layer of papier mâché around the frame you can squeeze the excess water from the pulp and mould it into a distressed and dented shape. Cherubs like the ones used here are easy to find, especially around Christmas time or from specialist shops. Once it has been sprayed gold, no one will guess how your frame used to look.

MATERIALS YOU WILL NEED

Newspaper
Large plastic container
Wallpaper paste
Plain picture frame
Glue
Plastic cherubs
Gold spray paint

1 Tear up narrow strips of newspaper and place in a container. Mix up some wallpaper paste and add it to the container, mixing it well with your hands. Squeeze out the excess moisture and apply the gluey mixture to the frame, building up layers until you achieve the desired effect.

2 Leave the papier mâché to dry overnight. Glue the cherubs to the frame using a strong adhesive. When dry, spray the frame gold.

Découpage Frame

Découpage is a technique used to decorate a surface by applying to it illustrations that have been cut from other sources. It was an enormously popular pastime in the Victorian era when all kinds of objects, large and small, were covered in delightful pictures. You can find suitable images for découpage in magazines, on wrapping paper and from similar sources.

MATERIALS YOU WILL NEED

Plain frame
Cardboard
Ruler
Craft knife
Découpage images
Paint
Glue
Spray varnish

1 Lay the frame on a piece of cardboard and trace around it, leaving a good margin all round. Cut it out. Make the gap in the centre slightly smaller than that of the original frame.

2 Carefully cut out the images you are going to use. Paint the cardboard frame in a colour that will enhance the découpage pieces. When dry, glue the cardboard frame to the original one.

3 Arrange the découpage pieces on the frame until you are happy with the composition. Glue the pieces down so that they slightly overlap each other. When you have finished the découpage, spray lightly with a matte varnish to seal the surface.

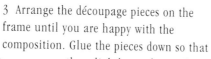

This découpage card is typically Victorian in style, but your theme can be as modern or as traditional as you like. If you need to repeat a picture, simply make copies of it on a colour photocopier. Turn to page 72 for instructions on how to make a basic card.

Funky Frame

This is the quickest and easiest way to jazz up a plain frame. Invent your own shape, or use the template at the back of the book. When you cut it out, make sure that the cardboard frame is wider than the original one so that it completely hides it. If you get bored with your cardboard frame, you can always peel it off and design a new one.

MATERIALS YOU WILL NEED

Cardboard
Scissors or craft knife
Glue
Plain frame
Poster paint
Glitter

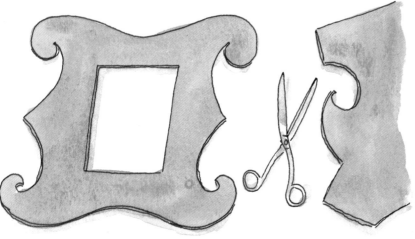

2 Paint the cardboard frame the colour of your choice. When dry, apply glue in small areas then sprinkle glitter over these. Leave to dry and gently blow away the excess glitter.

1 Trace the template from the back of the book and enlarge it by photocopying to the appropriate size for your frame. Cut out the cardboard shape and glue this to the front of the frame.

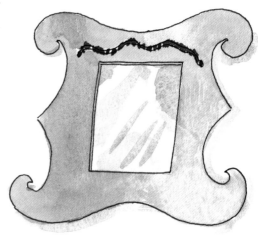

HANDMADE BOOKS

Cherub Album

This charming book was inspired by a friend with a new baby. It is a special scrapbook whose blank pages can be filled with cards, photographs, notes and precious keepsakes. The album is simple to make and, for added luxury, it can be wrapped in clouds of gold and white tissue paper and kept in a gilded box. Use baby footprints, trumpets and musical notes to stamp cards, wrapping paper and even some of the pages in the book.

MATERIALS YOU WILL NEED

Decorative white paper
Plain-paged book
Gold ribbon
Ruler
Glue
Gold paper
Spray adhesive
Plastic cherubs
White feathers

1 Using a decorative white paper, cover the book following the method shown on page 52. Make a slit in the front cover and thread through a length of ribbon. Glue the end in place inside the book. Repeat for the back cover.

2 Measure the area between the inside front cover and the outer edge of the first page. Cut a piece of gold paper this size. Spray the paper with adhesive, then fix it carefully into the book. Repeat the process for the back of the book.

3 Measure the spine of the book, then cut a strip of gold paper that is slightly longer and three times as wide as the spine. Use spray adhesive to fix the paper to the spine, carefully tucking the ends in top and bottom. Glue the cherubs to the front cover, adding soft feathers for wings.

t's fun to decorate a few pages inside the album. Make a stencil of your chosen design (there are templates at the back of the book), then use a sponge to dab gold paint through the stencil to make the print. Remember not to overload the sponge with paint, or you might find that it seeps under the stencil.

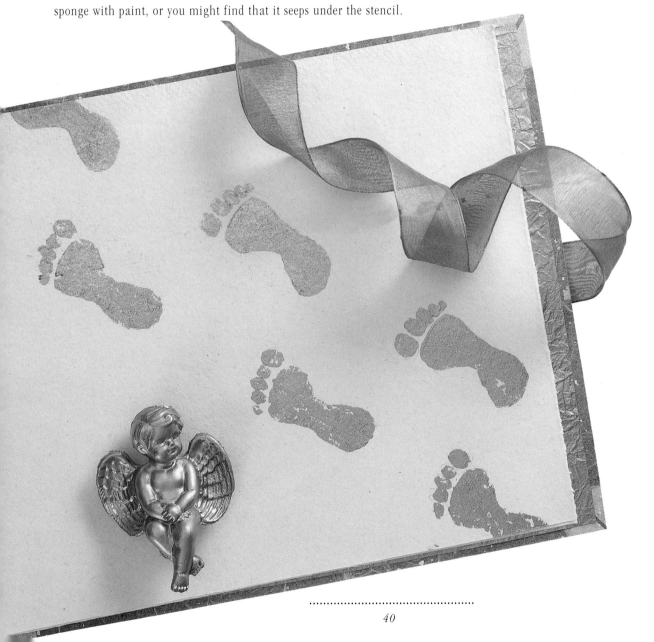

Book for a Cook

This book is perfect for someone who collects recipes and never knows where to keep them. Tear or cut cartridge paper into as many pages as necessary, then cut two pieces of acetate to exactly the same size. Acetate covers are ideal for recipe books as they protect them from dirty fingers.

Measure and mark the place for punching holes. Do a few pages at a time, then use the new holes to mark exactly where the next ones should be punched. The spoon and knife are simple stencils sprayed with silver paint, and the fork is glued in place then bound into the page. You can, of course, replace the real fork with a stencil.

MATERIALS YOU WILL NEED

Cartridge paper
Acetate
Hole punch
Silver paint
Fork
Glue
String

molluscus

Echinoidea

Ascidiacea

crambe maritima

laminar

Seaside Scrapbook

Collect and store mementos of special days in a simple scrapbook. This one has an ocean theme, but you can make a scrapbook to suit any occasion. Begin by punching holes in some loose sheets of coarsely made paper and binding them together with raffia. Don't tie the raffia too tightly, or you'll find it difficult to open the book and turn the pages. Position your treasures to create a pleasing composition and don't be tempted to glue anything down until you are happy with the whole page.

If you have a favourite poem about the sea, or a story that reminds you of days spent at the beach, make room for these too.

MATERIALS YOU WILL NEED

Hole punch
Handmade paper
Raffia

Book for a Lover

This is a fun and funky present for your loved one. The extremely kitsch pink fur fabric gives the whole thing a rather light-hearted feel, but any handmade gift is always a special token of affection. Two squares of card are sprayed gold and the fur heart is simply stuck on top. The book is then bound together by threading some matching ribbon through holes punched in the cover and pages.

MATERIALS YOU WILL NEED

Scissors or craft knife
Card
Gold spray
Paper
Ruler
Hole punch
Fur fabric
Glue
Ribbon

1   Cut two squares of card to be the front and back covers of your book. Spray both pieces gold.

2   Measure and tear sheets of paper to make pages for the book. Use a ruler to get rough edges.

3   Use a hole punch to make two evenly spaced holes in each piece of card. Place the sheets of paper between the pieces of card and mark the holes with a pencil. Make holes where the marks are.

4   Using the template at the back of the book, cut out a heart shape from fake fur. Glue this to the gold side of a piece of card, making sure that the holes remain on the left-hand side.

5   Place the pages between the pieces of card and line up all the holes. Thread pieces of ribbon through the holes and knot them to hold the book together.

Valentine's Card

To make this Valentine's card, tear pink tissue paper into tiny pieces and mix it with a little water and wallpaper paste to make papier mâché. Using the template at the back of the book, draw a heart on a piece of paper. Spread the pulp thinly over the heart shape, then leave to dry flat. Glue the heart to a paler coloured piece of tissue paper. Using a paintbrush, carefully draw water around the heart shape, leaving a thin margin all round. The wet tissue will tear away leaving you with a pretty, soft edge around the heart. Mount this on to a piece of gold paper, and in turn mount this on to a piece of thick paper folded in half to form a card.

MATERIALS YOU WILL NEED

Pink and white tissue paper
Wallpaper paste
Pencil
Paper
Glue
Paintbrush
Gold paper

Gold Moon and Silver Star Books

These books make great gifts. The moon and star are made from papier mâché, then transferred when dry to the front of the books. Make the papier mâché figures on a piece of paper on which you have drawn the outline of the shape. (You will find instructions on how to make papier mâché on page 30.) It is important to leave the papier mâché shapes to dry somewhere flat. If they are left on an uneven surface, you will find that the dry shapes have become distorted and won't lie flat on the book covers. Paint the shapes and leave to dry thoroughly before gluing them to the front cover.

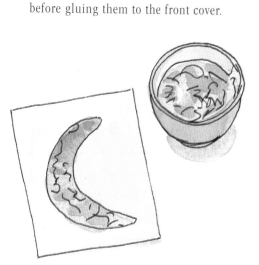

1 Using the templates at the back of the book, copy your chosen design on to a piece of paper and mould the papier mâché pulp inside the outline. When dry, paint in gold or silver.

2 Cut two pieces of card the same size for the front and back cover of the book, then measure and tear sheets of paper to make pages. Scrunch up a piece of tissue paper until it is heavily textured, then use it to cover the two pieces of card. Make holes in the card and paper as described on page 45.

3 Glue the papier mâché shape to the book cover. Thread ribbons through the holes to join the pages and the covers. Instead of ribbon, why not use string sprayed to match the colour of the papier mâché shape?

Decorated Book, Pencils and Pencil Holder

Transform ordinary hardback notebooks into beautiful presents by covering them with decorated paper. Personalise them by using paper you have stamped or stencilled with names or initials, and add decorative endpapers and pretty page markers of twine or ribbon. Accompany notebooks with pencils and pencil holders covered with the same paper.

For a really special present, look for tatty secondhand books by favourite authors and re-cover to give them a unique quality and a new lease of life.

Covering pencils is a great way to use up odd scraps of paper left over from larger projects. The pencils are quick to make and will brighten any desk, particularly when grouped in a box decorated in a complementary paper.

MATERIALS YOU WILL NEED

BOOK
Decorative paper
Hardback book
Ruler
Scissors or craft knife
Double-sided tape

PENCILS
Uncut pencils, all the same size
Thin paper
Ruler
Scissors or craft knife
Glue

HOLDER
Pencil
Glass tumber
Cardboard
Scissors or craft knife
Masking tape
Decorative paper
Glue

Book

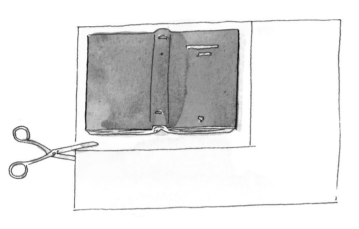

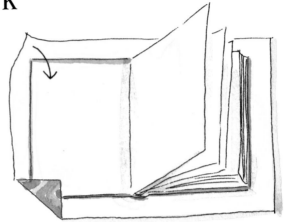

1 Place the paper face down on a flat surface and lay the open book on it, cover side up. Using a ruler, draw a straight line around the book, leaving a margin of about 2.5 cm (1 in). Cut out the rectangle you have drawn.

2 Place the book on the paper and open it to reveal the front cover. Fold the paper into the outer corners of the cover and attach it with double-sided tape.

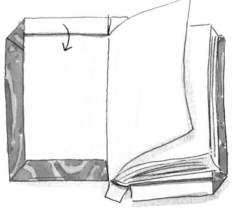

3 Fold the paper over the side of the book and attach it inside the cover with more tape. Hold the book open at 90° and stick down the paper along the corners and sides of the back cover.

4 Close the book and make a vertical snip in the paper on each side of the spine at the top and bottom of the book. Open the book again and attach the remaining flaps of paper to the front and back covers with more tape.

5 Using the end of a metal teaspoon, tuck the last pieces of paper down into the spine of the book.

Pencils

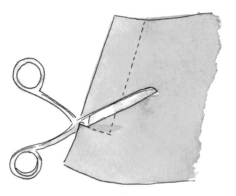

1 Place an uncut pencil on the short edge of a piece of paper. Measure and mark the exact length of the pencil and two-and-a-half times its width.

2 Cut out the rectangle of paper you have drawn and use it as a template for the other pencils.

3 Spread glue on the wrong side of the paper. Lay a pencil at one edge of the paper and carefully wrap it, making sure that the paper fits exactly.

4 When the pencil has dried, use a sharp knife to sharpen the point. (A pencil sharpener may tear the paper covering.)

Pencil Holder

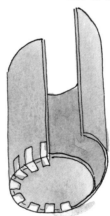

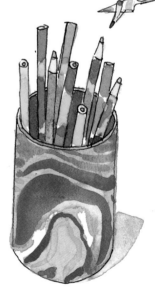

1 Trace around a glass on to a piece of cardboard, then cut out the shape. This will be the base of the pencil holder.

2 Measure the circumference of the disk, then cut a piece of cardboard 1 cm (½ in) longer than this and three-quarters the length of the average pencil. Tape the cardboard to the base.

3 Cover the finished pencil holder with a colourful paper, such as one you have printed, spattered, or marbled yourself.

DECORATIVE DESIGNS

Heart-shaped Box

This is a box to give to someone special, or in which to keep your own treasures safe. Use the heart template at the back of the book to give you the shape of the box, then decorate it according to your imagination. If you don't have an old key, cover the box with a fake fur heart, or attach heart-shaped chocolates wrapped in shiny paper.

MATERIALS YOU WILL NEED

Scissors or craft knife
Corrugated cardboard
Tape measure
Ruler
Masking tape
Spray adhesive
Coloured paper
An old key
Glue
Gold paint

1 Using the template, cut two heart shapes from corrugated cardboard to form the base and lid of the box. The base should be 3mm (⅛ in) smaller all round than the lid.

2 With a tape measure, measure around the outside edge of the lid. Alternatively, wind a piece of string around the circumference, then measure that against a ruler.

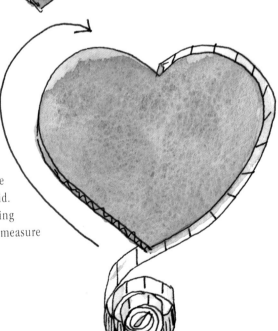

3 Decide the height you want the box to be, then cut out two strips of cardboard. Make one strip two-thirds wider than the other and both 1 cm (½ in) longer than the measurement of the outside edge of the lid. Tape the wider strip to the smaller heart to form the base of the box. The corrugations should be on the inside. Trim the cardboard where the strips overlap, then secure firmly with tape. Repeat for the lid.

5 Using spray adhesive, stick the coloured paper to the sides of the base and the lid. Make small snips in the paper when tucking under the overlap at the top and bottom of the box to create a smoother finish. Stick the paper hearts to the base and lid of the box.

6 Decorate the top of the box with a paper heart made from a different coloured paper and an old key that you have painted gold.

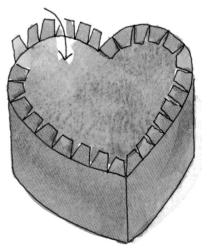

4 Trace around the lid and the base on to coloured paper and cut out the shapes. Cut two further strips of paper slightly longer and wider than the sides of the box and lid.

Oval Box

Handmade boxes make a refreshing alternative to giftwrapping when you want to give someone a special present; in fact, they are so pretty they are almost a present in themselves. Use them around your home, too, for serving homemade fudge, or simply for storing odds and ends. Basic boxes are very easy to make, and you will find templates at the back of the book for this and the Heart-shaped Box.

This oval box is perfect to fill with gorgeous chocolates layered between sheets of tissue paper. To make it, simply follow the method given on pages 56 and 57.

Remember that you can cover boxes that you have at home – such as shoe boxes – in the same way as you would a box you have made yourself. Turn to Steps 5 and 6 on page 57 for tips on how to achieve a perfect finish.

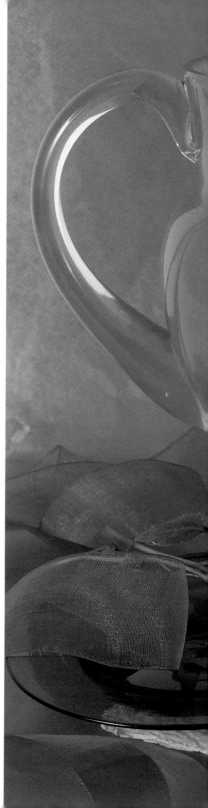

MATERIALS YOU WILL NEED

Scissors or craft knife
Corrugated cardboard
Tape measure
Rule
Masking tape
Spray adhesive
Decorative paper

Gift Bags

Another alternative to decorative boxes and pretty giftwrapping is to make these simple bags. Choose a paper that folds easily, but which is not too flimsy, and line the bags with tissue paper to complement their colours. The bags can be used to carry confetti on a wedding day, or filled with sweets to give to children at the end of a birthday party.

2 Using the broken lines as a guide, fold in the sides of the bag.

3 Turn the bag upside down and make a base for it by folding in the sides. Fold over the flaps and glue them securely in position. You will find it helps to place one hand inside the bag as you are pressing down the glued area.

4 Using a hole punch, make two holes in the same place on each side of the bag. Thread lengths of ribbon through to make handles.

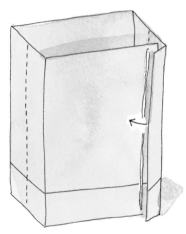

1 Copy the template from the end of the book on to a piece of thick paper. Fold the paper away from you along the horizontal line then straighten it again. Using the printed vertical lines as a guide, fold the paper around and glue down the edge.

Wedding Giftwrap

Beautifully wrapped presents are always admired. This one is perfect for a wedding gift. A plain box is wrapped in tissue paper, tied with a raffia bow, and decorated with tissue-paper rose petals. Because the paper petals are tinted with watercolour paint, they take on a nice crinkled effect reminiscent of the real thing.

MATERIALS YOU WILL NEED

Plain box
Pink tissue paper
Scissors or craft knife
Tape
Raffia
Watercolour paints
Glue

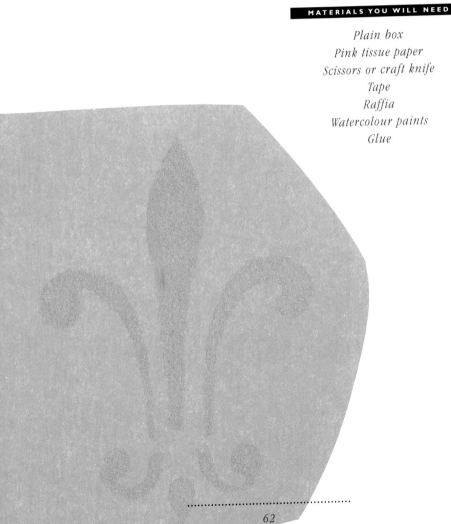

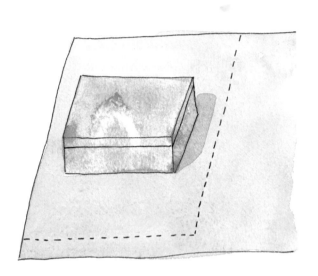

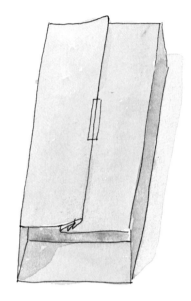

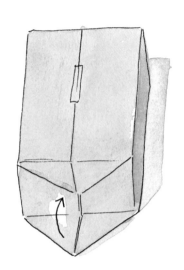

1 Place the gift box on the pink tissue paper and trim it so that the paper just overlaps on top and at the sides. (Too much paper will make the folds clumsy and bulky.)

2 Take the two long sides of the paper and fold them together as tight to the gift box as possible. Fold over again so that no raw edges of paper are showing, and use a small piece of tape to secure the ends.

3 Fold the sides into the middle at each end of the box and secure with a small piece of tape. Repeat with the top and bottom flaps.

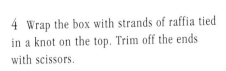

4 Wrap the box with strands of raffia tied in a knot on the top. Trim off the ends with scissors.

5 Cut out petal shapes in tissue paper. Concertina the tissue so that you can cut several petals at once.

6 Dab the petals with watercolour paint and leave to dry. Glue the petals in a random fashion to the giftwrapped box.

Rose Napkins and Place Settings

Use the stencilling technique explained on page 27 to turn plain paper napkins into something delightful. Choose simple motifs that lend themselves to the occasion, such as a heart for a romantic dinner for two, or a baby's footprint for a christening. When the stencil pattern has dried, roll up each napkin and tie it with a ribbon.

MATERIALS YOU WILL NEED

Plain paper napkin
Stencil
Paint
Ribbon

Rose place settings add the perfect touch to any wedding dining table. You will need some white card, pale tissue paper and dried rose buds, which are available from dried flower specialists. Glue a small piece of tissue to each card then fix the rose buds in place with a couple of a stitches. Write the name of each guest inside a card and place it on the table.

Blue Flower Card and Tag

Handmade paper can be used to make unique cards and gift tags to accompany stylishly wrapped gift boxes. To make a greetings card, first fold the handmade paper in two. If you find it difficult to fold, place a ruler where you would like the fold to be and gently score a line with a blunt knife. If the handmade paper is very absorbent, line the card with tissue paper on to which you have written your message. Decorate the front of the card with a delicate flower paper.

To make a tag, cut out a label shape from the flower paper and make a hole in the curved end with a hole punch. Use a ribbon to attach the tag to the parcel.

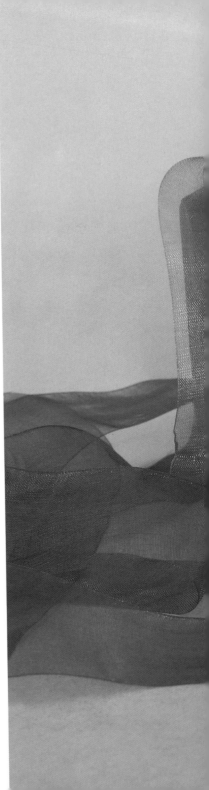

MATERIALS YOU WILL NEED

CARD
Handmade paper
Ruler
Blunt knife
Tissue paper
Handmade flower paper

TAG
Scissors or craft knife
Handmade flower paper
Hole punch
Ribbon

Spoon Place Settings

Spoon place settings are a great idea for a children's tea party. Inexpensive plastic spoons are instantly transformed with a colourful tag tied on with a matching ribbon. To make them extra-special, dip each spoon in melted chocolate and leave to set before attaching the tags. Use thick paper or thin card for each tag, choosing colours that complement those of the spoons.

MATERIALS YOU WILL NEED

Thick paper or thin card
Scissors or craft knife
Hole punch
Ribbon
Spoon

Envelope and
Ribbon Greetings Card

Everyone loves to receive handmade cards, and they are surprisingly quick and easy to make. The finishing touch is the made-to-measure envelope. Either use the template at the back of the book, or open up an envelope you already have and draw around it. It is generally a good idea to make the envelope first; that way you can ensure that the card fits.

The parcel on the opposite page is wrapped in green tissue paper that was first stencilled in Latin script. To make the stencil, trace the outline of the letters on card or acetate and cut them out with a craft knife. Making a calligraphy stencil is more intricate and takes a little more time than cutting a simple shape, such as the heart on page 27, but the end result is worth the effort.

MATERIALS YOU WILL NEED

ENVELOPE

Coloured paper
Pencil
Scissors or craft knife
Glue
Sealing wax
Coin

CARD

Handmade paper
Tissue paper
Ribbon

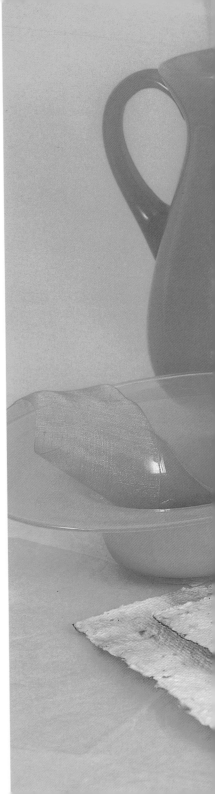

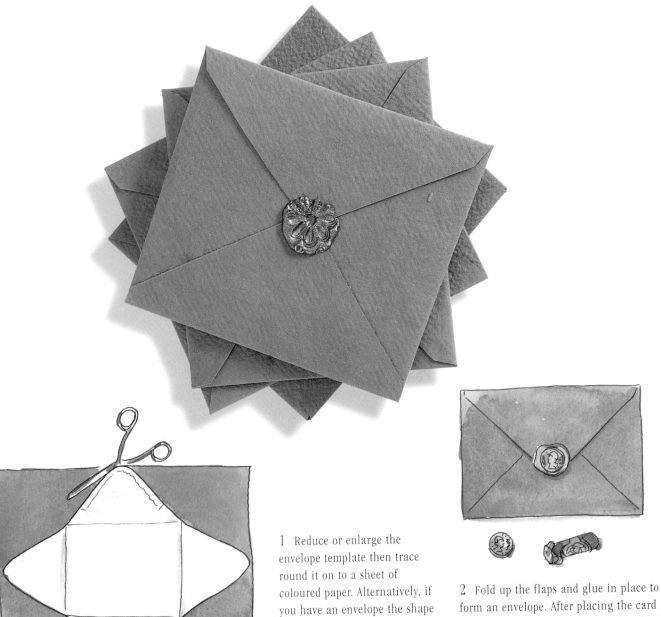

1 Reduce or enlarge the envelope template then trace round it on to a sheet of coloured paper. Alternatively, if you have an envelope the shape you need, open it out, draw around it, and adjust the size in the same way.

2 Fold up the flaps and glue in place to form an envelope. After placing the card inside, decorate the envelope with a drop of sealing wax stamped with any small patterned object, such as a coin or a ring.

1 Make up a basic card using handmade paper. You will find that tearing along a fold gives a more natural finish than cutting with scissors. Fold the paper in half and decorate it with a piece of coloured tissue paper.

2 Place a length of ribbon inside the card and tie into a bow at the spine of the card.

Scrolls

A colourful paper scroll lined with tissue paper and fastened with sealing wax and a bow, makes an unusual and eye-catching party invitation. Sealing wax is available from shops that sell arts and crafts materials.

MATERIALS YOU WILL NEED

Handmade paper
Ruler
Tissue paper
Scissors or craft knife
Glue
Ribbon
Sealing wax
Coin

1 Tear the handmade paper into rectangles about 20 x 15 cm (8 x 6 in). Cut the tissue paper into slightly smaller rectangles. Write your message on the tissue paper, then fix it to the larger piece of paper with a little glue.

2 Roll the paper into a scroll with the tissue paper innermost. Tie a length of ribbon around the scroll to hold it together. Melt some sealing wax on the edge and press a coin into it to make an attractive pattern and keep the scroll closed.

Pink Berry and Mistletoe Place Settings

These place settings with their colourful winter berries and sprigs of mistletoe would be ideal for a Christmas dinner. Follow the instructions for the Rose Place Setting on page 65, adding decoration to suit the event.

MATERIALS YOU WILL NEED

Handmade or art paper
Tissue paper
Glue
Berries

Blue, Gold and Silver Cards

aking your own greetings cards not only brings pleasure to the recipients, it can save you quite a lot of money too. Decide on the shape of the card and the design of the decorative detail – whether printed or stencilled – and set up a mini production line. You'll find that you can produce a great many cards fairly quickly. Refer to page 73 for information on how to make a basic greetings card. At the back of the book there is a selection of stencil patterns. The star and the crowns pictured opposite are evocative of Christmas, but the golden sun would be appropriate for many different celebrations. Stencil the tissue paper and allow it to dry before cutting out the section you need and fixing it to the card with tiny drops of glue.

MATERIALS YOU WILL NEED

Handmade or art paper
Tissue paper
Stencil
Metallic paint
Glue

Dancing People Garlands

U se these colourful paper garlands to add the finishing touches to celebration parties and dinners. Hang the dancing girls and boys across the backs of chairs at children's parties, or loop the garlands across dinner tables and doorways. Use the same technique to make simple greetings cards: Christmas trees, Easter bunnies and garlands of flowers for Mother's Day all work well.

MATERIALS YOU WILL NEED

Soft pencil
Tracing paper
Thick coloured paper
Scissors or craft knife

1 Using a soft pencil, trace your chosen design on to a piece of tracing paper. Place the tracing paper, pencil side down, on the edge of the sheet of coloured paper and transfer the design to it.

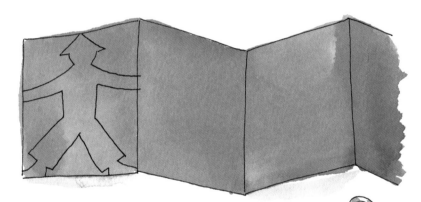

2 Make your first fold exactly on the edge of the design, then continue to concertina-fold the paper as many times as you can. It is very important that the design fits perfectly on to the width of the folded paper.

3 Taking care not to break the folded edges, cut out the design. To make a longer garland, repeat the process with further pieces of paper joined together at the ends.

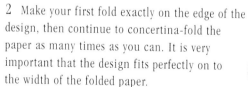

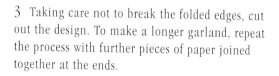

Tissue Paper Bunting

This multi-coloured bunting looks particularly pretty when used outdoors at summer parties. It is best to cut out all of the flag shapes first, using a pattern to ensure that they are the same size. If you make a stack of tissue paper, you can cut several pieces at a time.

MATERIALS YOU WILL NEED

Ruler
Cardboard
Tissue paper in assorted colours
Scissors or craft knife
Glue
Coloured string

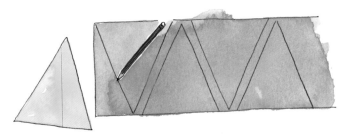

1 Using a ruler, measure and draw a triangle roughly 12 x 14 x 14 cm (4¾ x 5 x 5 in) on a piece of cardboard. Cut out the triangle and use it as your template. Trace around the template on the tissue paper and cut out the triangles you have drawn.

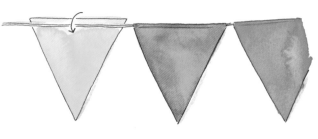

2 Spread a narrow strip of glue along the shortest edge of the triangle. Lay the string just under the glue and fold the paper over the string. Repeat, leaving a regular gap between the triangles.

TEMPLATES

The following templates are taken from projects in this book, and are there to inspire you to create your own designs. Page numbers are given when the design is featured in a particular project. Use a photocopier to enlarge or reduce the patterns to fit the card or paper you are decorating. Ideas for designs can be found anywhere: upholstery fabrics, wallpaper, wrapping paper, and features in magazines are particularly good sources.

Crowns, page 77

Starfish

Fleur-de-lys

Leaf design

Sun, page 77

Musical notes
and trumpet

Leaf design

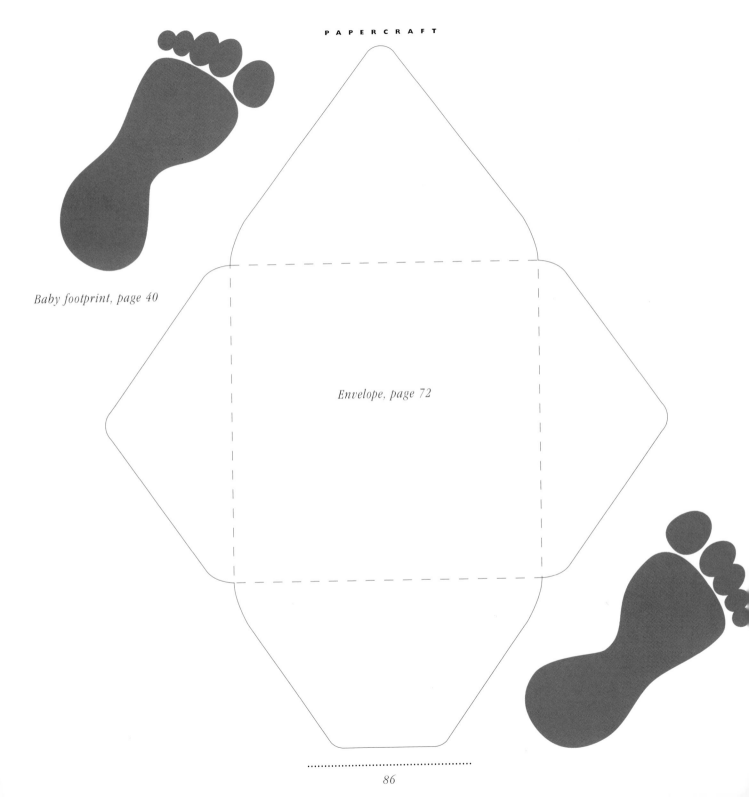

Baby footprint, page 40

Envelope, page 72

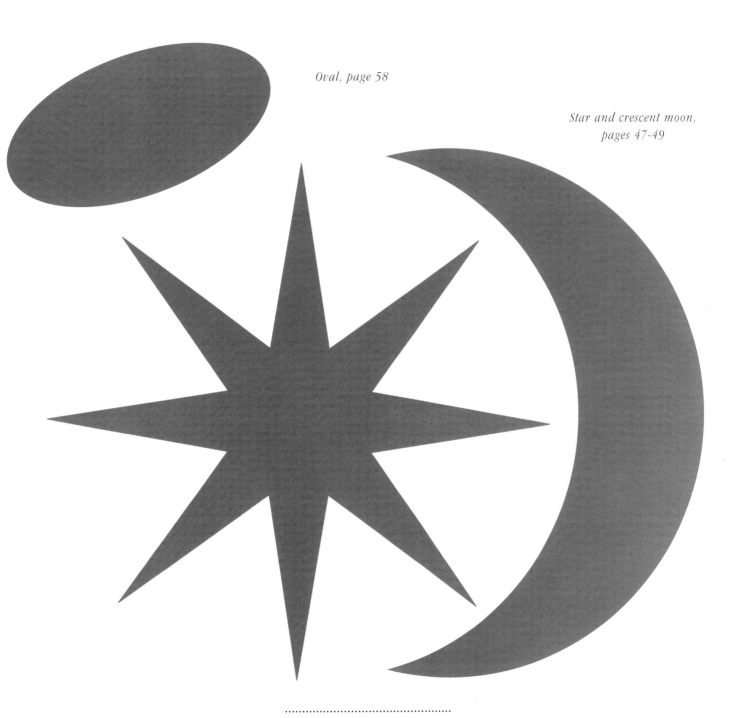

Oval, page 58

Star and crescent moon,
pages 47-49

Rose, page 65

Dancing figure, page 78

*Heart, pages 24, 27,
44, 46, 56*

Spoon and fork, page 41

Frame, page 34

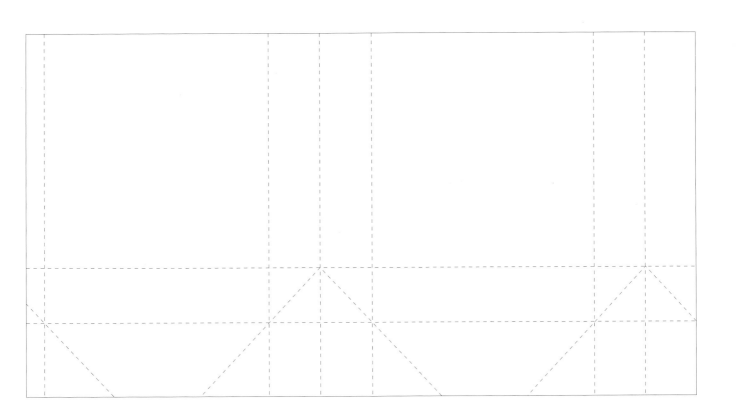

Gift bag, page 61

Suppliers

Most of the items used to make the projects in this book can be found at local stationers, art and crafts shops and large department stores. You might also like to contact the following companies, some of whom will supply materials by mail order.

Atlantis Art Materials

146 Brick Lane

London E1 6RU

Tel: 0171-377 8855

Suppliers of art and crafts materials. Mail order.

Daler-Rowney

12 Percy Street

London W1A 2BP

Tel: 0171-636 8241

Suppliers of art and crafts materials. Mail order.

Falkiner Fine Papers Ltd

76 Southampton Row

London WC1B 4AR

Tel: 0171-831 1151

Suppliers of specialist papers; tools and equipment.

T.N. Lawrence & Son Ltd

117-119 Clerkenwell Road

London EC1R 4AR

Tel: 0171-242 3534

Suppliers of paper and artists' materials. Mail order.

Paperchase Products Ltd

213 Tottenham Court Road

London W1P 9AF

Tel: 0171-580 8496

Suppliers of papers, boards, acetate and adhesives.

Reeves Art Shop

178 Kensington High Street

London W8 7RG

Tel: 0171-937 5370

Suppliers of art and crafts materials.

Specialist Crafts

PO Box 247

Leicester LE1 9QS

Tel: 0116 251 0405

Suppliers of moulds and deckles. Mail order.